Enrichment

MATH

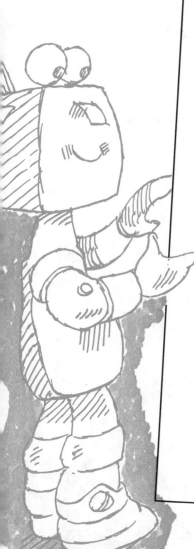

Dear Student,

Here is your very own *Enrichment Math* book. This book is filled with exciting things to do for fun at home. Sometimes you will play games. Sometimes you will have contests. Sometimes you will search for special things in your house. Your Mom, Dad, or another grown-up will help you and play with you.

While you are having fun, you will be learning math. We hope *Enrichment Math* will be one of your favorite things this year.

Good luck from your friends at *Enrichment Math.*

Peggy Kaye

Carole Greenes

Linda Schulman

Table of Contents

My House

Tell about your house.

My house has _____ beds.

My house has _____ doors.

My house has _____ bananas.

My house has _____ elephants.

My house has _____ sinks.

My Family

Draw a family picture.
Have a grown-up help you.

How many people are in your picture? _____
Have a grown-up write their names.
You write the number of letters.

Mom _____ 3__ _____ ____

_____ _____ _____ _____

_____ _____ _____ _____

_____ _____ _____ _____

Writing Numbers

Hunt for Numbers

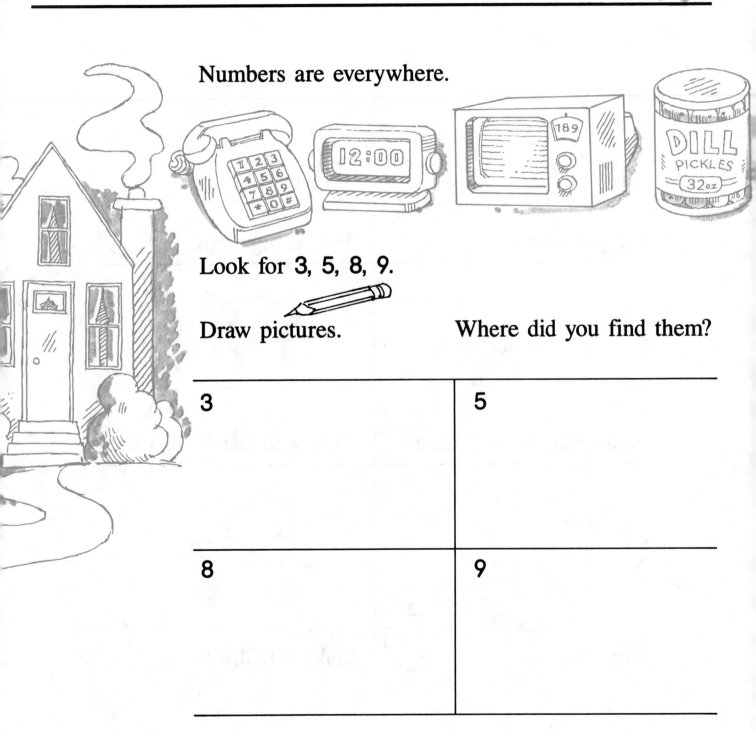

Numbers are everywhere.

Look for **3, 5, 8, 9.**

Draw pictures.   Where did you find them?

3	5
8	9

Can You Do It?

Try to do it.

Ask a grown-up to check your counting.

Draw a smile on the button if you did it.

Jump **3** times.

Take **8** big steps.

Touch your nose **6** times.

Clap your hands **15** times.

Hop **13** times.

Make **10** silly faces.

Counting from 1 to 15

Here Is Your Zoo

Draw more elephants, snakes, birds, and monkeys in your zoo.

My zoo has _____ elephants.

My zoo has _____ snakes.

My zoo has _____ monkeys.

My zoo has _____ birds.

Counting Path

Play this game with a grown-up.

You need a coin.

1. Put the coin on START.

2. Take turns moving the coin on the path.
You can move 1, 2, or 3 spaces.

3. The person who gets the coin to FINISH wins.

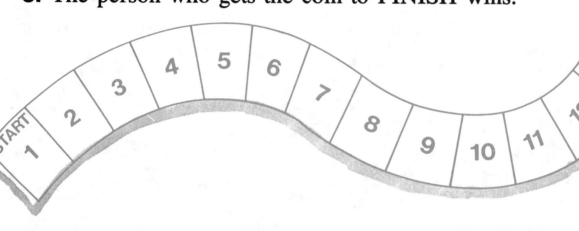

Who won? _____

Play again.

Who won? _____

Make your own number path.
Make it longer. Make it go to **20** or more.
Play the game on your path.

Numbers to 20 and Solving Nonroutine Problems

Letters, Letters, Letters

You can count letters.

Count every v on this page. How many? _____

Count every y on this page. How many? _____

Count every v and every y. How many? _____

Count every w on this page. How many? _____

Count every v and every w How many? _____

My Name

Do this with a grown-up.

My first name is _____ .

My first name has _____ letters.

My last name is _____ .

My last name has _____ letters.
Count these letters in your name.

a ____   e ____   i ____   o ____   u ____

Color a box for each **a**, **e**, **i**, **o**, and **u** in your name.

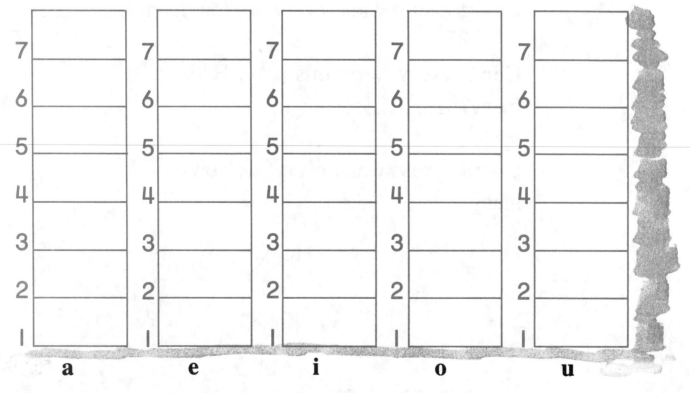

Which has more?   **a   e   i   o   u**

Counting, Graphing, and Comparing Numbers

Spoons, Forks, Knives

Count in your kitchen.

Count spoons.

____ spoons

Count forks.

____ forks

Count knives.

____ knives

Ring the answer.

I have more   or

I have more   or

I have more   or

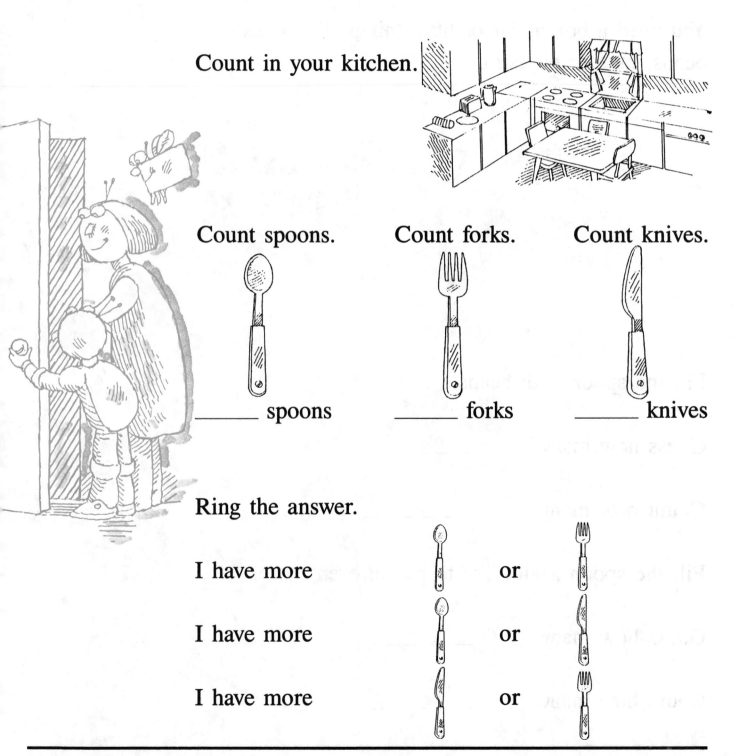

Fill the Spoon

Play this with a grown-up.

You need a tablespoon.

You need a box or jar of little things, like dried beans, nuts or popcorn.

Fill the spoon with beans.

Guess how many.   _____

Count how many.   _____

Fill the spoon again. Try to put in even more!

Guess how many.   _____

Count how many.   _____

The Stick Family

This is a stick dad.	Draw a stick mom.	Draw a stick boy.	Draw a stick girl.

The stick family has _____ feet.

The stick family has _____ eyes.

The stick family has _____ arms.

The stick family has _____ fingers.

The stick family has _____ tails.

How many are there in your family?

_____ feet _____ eyes _____ arms _____ fingers

Name Writing Contest

Do this with a grown-up.

Color the boxes with these numbers: 5, 10, 15, 20, 25, 30, 35, 40, 45, 50, 55, 60, 65, 70, 75, 80, 85, 90, 95, 100.

1	2	3	4	5	6	7	8	9	10
11	12	13	14	15	16	17	18	19	20
21	22	23	24	25	26	27	28	29	30
31	32	33	34	35	36	37	38	39	40
41	42	43	44	45	46	47	48	49	50
51	52	53	54	55	56	57	58	59	60
61	62	63	64	65	66	67	68	69	70
71	72	73	74	75	76	77	78	79	80
81	82	83	84	85	86	87	88	89	90
91	92	93	94	95	96	97	98	99	100

Do you see a pattern? _____

Have your grown-up count by fives to 100.

Write your name as often as you can while he counts.

How many times did you write your name? _____

Counting by Fives

Circles and Squares

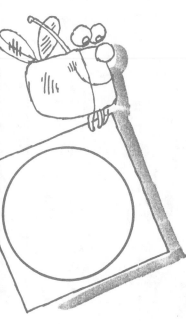

☐   ◯

Draw 10 squares in each circle.

◯   ◯   ◯

◯

How many circles? _____   ☐ How many squares? _____

☐

Draw 6 more squares here.

☐

How many squares now? _____

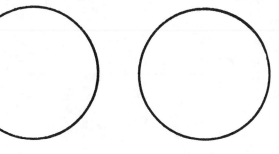 **Draw** 10 dots in each circle.

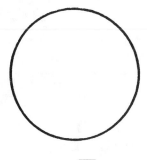

◯   ◯   ◯   ◯

◯ How many circles? _____   ● How many dots? _____

Count Up Time

Ask a grown-up to help you.

You need many things like dried beans or paper clips.

1	2	3	4	5	6
7	8	9	10	11	12

Put 1 bean in box 1.

Put 2 beans in box 2.

Put 3 beans in box 3, and so on up to box 12.

Count all the beans. How many in all? _____

Lots of Stars

10 stars are in a cloud.

Put 10 more in a cloud.

Put 10 more in a cloud.

Put 10 more in a cloud.

How many clouds? _____

How many stars? _____

Circle Them Up

Do this with a grown-up.

You need some little things, like dried beans or paper clips.

Count 19 beans.

Put 4 beans in each circle. Put the left-over beans in the triangle.

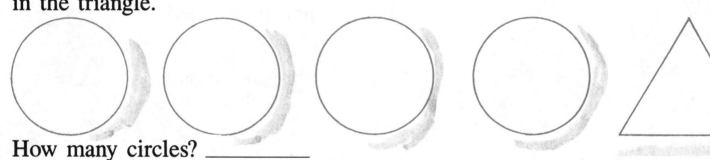

How many circles? _____

How many beans are in the triangle? _____

Do it again. This time put 10 beans in the circle. Put the left-over beans in the triangle.

How many circles? _____

How many beans are in the triangle? _____

LESSON
9

Money Road

Count the money on the road.

How many cents? _____ ¢

Count the money on this road.

How many cents? _____ ¢

Count the money on this road.

How many cents? _____ ¢

Pick Your Money Road

Play this game with a grown-up.

There are 4 money roads.

Pick a road. Count the money. How many cents? _____ ¢

Your grown-up picks a road. How many cents? _____ ¢

Who got the most money? _____
has

Play again. Pick a different road.

Who got the most money this time? _____
has

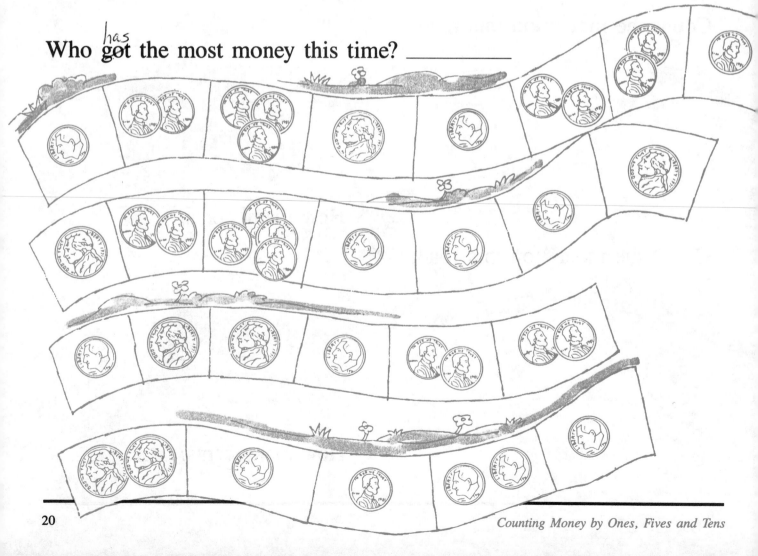

Counting Money by Ones, Fives and Tens

Dominoes

LESSON 10

How many dots in all?

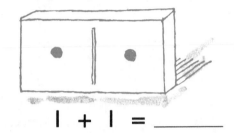

1 + 1 = _____

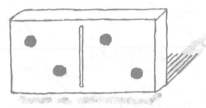

2 + 2 = _____

$$\begin{array}{r} 3 \\ +\ 3 \\ \hline \end{array}$$

$$\begin{array}{r} 4 \\ +\ 4 \\ \hline \end{array}$$

4 + 4 = _____

3 + 3 = _____

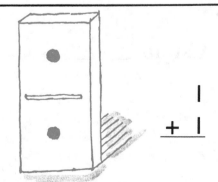

$$\begin{array}{r} 1 \\ +\ 1 \\ \hline \end{array}$$

$$\begin{array}{r} 2 \\ +\ 2 \\ \hline \end{array}$$

Target Game

Play this game with a grown-up.

Toss a coin or a paper clip on the game board.

Write the number.

Toss again.

Write the number.

Add the numbers.

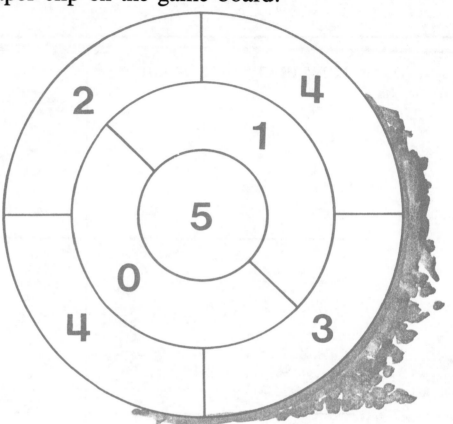

My score   My grown-up's score

Toss **1** _____   Toss **1** _____

Toss **2** _____   Toss **2** _____

Add up _____   Add up _____

Who won? _____

Play again. Who won? _____

The Color of 5

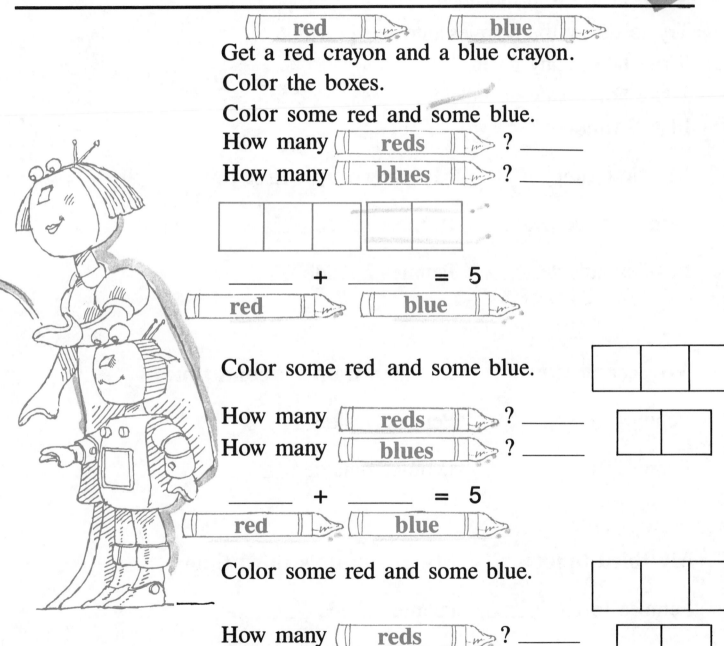

red   blue

Get a red crayon and a blue crayon.

Color the boxes.

Color some red and some blue.

How many **reds** ? _____

How many **blues** ? _____

_____ + _____ = 5

red   blue

Color some red and some blue.

How many **reds** ? _____

How many **blues** ? _____

_____ + _____ = 5

red   blue

Color some red and some blue.

How many **reds** ? _____

How many **blues** ? _____

_____ + _____ = 5

red   blue

5 in a Bowl

You need **5** pennies or **5** paper clips.
You also need a bowl.
Put the bowl on the floor.
Stand away from the bowl.
Try to throw the pennies into the bowl.
Write how many go inside.
Write how many go outside.
Play **3** times.

My first time

Pennies inside _____

Pennies outside _____

My grown-up's first time

Pennies inside _____

Pennies outside _____

My second time

Pennies inside _____

Pennies outside _____

My grown-up's second time

Pennies inside _____

Pennies outside _____

My third time

Pennies inside _____

Pennies outside _____

My grown-up's third time

Pennies inside _____

Pennies outside _____

Adding with Basic Facts: Sums of 5

Bug Zoo

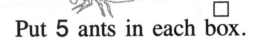

Here are ant boxes.

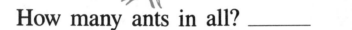

Put **5** ants in each box.

How many ants in all? _____ $5 + 5 =$ _____

Here are butterfly boxes.

Put **7** butterflies in each box.

How many butterflies in all? _____ $7 + 7 =$ _____

Here are spider boxes.

Put **9** spiders in each box.

How many spiders in all? _____ $9 + 9 =$ _____

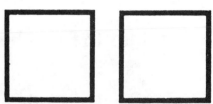
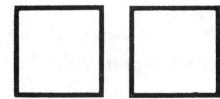

Number Ladder

Play this game with a grown-up.

Climb the number ladder.

Start at the bottom.

Add 1 to the number on each step.

If you make a mistake, you fall.

Then you must start over.

When you make it to the top,
put a ⌣ on the ⚆

Play again. Add **2** at each step.

Play again. Add **3** at each step.

Play again. Add **4** at each step.

The ladder, from top to bottom, shows: 7, 9, 6, 8, 4, 0, 2, 5, 1, 3

Housewot

How many sinks are in your house?
How many beds in your house?
How many in all?

+   =

_____   _____   _____
        in all

How many lions are in your house?
How many tigers?
How many in all?

+   =

_____   _____   _____
    in all

How many doors are in your house?
How many umbrellas are in your house?
How many in all?

+   =

_____   _____   _____
        in all

Emu the Robot

Work with a grown-up to fill in the numbers for
this story.

Emu is a good robot. He has magic flowers. He
has _____ magic red flowers and _____ magic
blue flowers. How many magic flowers in
all? _____

Emu goes for a walk. He meets _____ boys
and _____ girls.

How many boys and girls in all? _____

With his magic flowers, he gives the children some
birds. He gives them _____ redbirds
and _____ bluebirds. How many birds in
all? _____

2 birds fly away. How many birds now? _____

Emu must go home now.

He waves goodbye _____ times.

The children wave _____ times.

How many goodbye waves in all? _____

Emu walks _____ miles.

He runs _____ miles.

How many miles in all? _____

In The Box

Get some beans or other little things.

Put 2 here.

Put 3 here.

Put 3 here.

Put 2 here.

How many? _____

2 + 3 = _____

How many? _____

3 + 2 = _____

Put 4 here.

Put 5 here.

Put 5 here.

Put 4 here.

How many? _____

4 + 5 = _____

How many? _____

5 + 4 = _____

10 on Plates

Do this with a grown-up.

You need **10** pennies or paper clips.

You need **2** plates.

Put the **10** pennies on the **2** plates.

Here is one way to do it.   Here is another way.

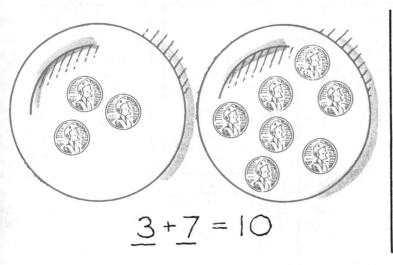

$$\underline{3} + \underline{7} = 10$$

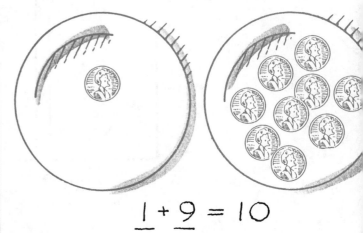

$$\underline{1} + \underline{9} = 10$$

Now use your pennies and plates. Try to find **6** new ways.

Write numbers to show what you did.

_____ + _____ = 10   _____ + _____ = 10

_____ + _____ = 10   _____ + _____ = 10

_____ + _____ = 10   _____ + _____ = 10

The Cover Up

Here are 10 circles.

Cover **2** circles. How many now? _____

Cover **8** circles. How many now? _____

Cover **6** circles. How many now? _____

Cover **4** circles. How many now? _____

Cover **3** circles. How many now? _____

Cover **7** circles. How many now? _____

Cover **5** circles. How many now? _____

Subtracting with Basic Facts: Sums of 10

What's Hiding?

Play this game with a grown-up.

You need 10 little things like beans, pennies, or paper clips.

Step 1 The grown-up puts some on a table. You count how many.

Step 2 Close your eyes. The grown-up takes some away.

Step 3 You open your eyes. Count how many are left.

Step 4 Tell how many are missing.

If you are right, you color a circle.

If you are wrong, the grown-up colors a circle.

Your circles: ○ ○ ○ ○ ○ ○

The grown-up's circles: ○ ○ ○ ○ ○ ○

Subtracting with Basic Facts

Hilda Hid It

Hilda is a funny robot.

Hilda hides things.

How many beds are in your house? _____

Hilda hides 1.

How many beds now?

_____ – 1 = _____

How many chairs are in your kitchen? _____

Hilda hides 2.

How many chairs now?

_____ – 2 = _____

How many coats are in your house? _____

Hilda hides 3.

How many coats now?

_____ – 3 = _____

How many towels are in your bathroom? _____

Hilda hides 1.

How many now?

_____ – 1 = _____

Lose and Win Game

Play this game with a grown-up.

You need **20** pennies or paper clips.

You take **10** and your grown-up takes **10**.

You also need something VERY small, like a bean.

Here is the game board.

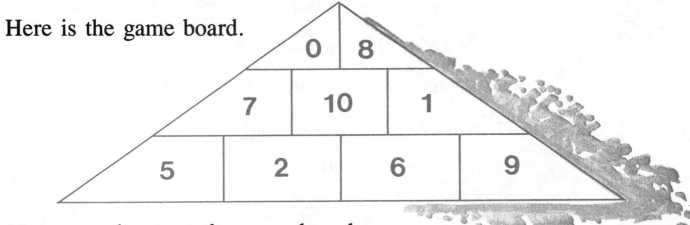

You toss a bean on the game board.

What number did you get? _____

Take away that many pennies from your penny pile.

How many pennies do you have left? _____

Your grown-up tosses a bean.

What number did your grown-up get? _____

Your grown-up takes away that many pennies.

How many pennies does your grown-up have
left? _____

Who has more pennies now? _____ Hooray, the
winner!

Play again. Who is the winner? _____

Tic-Tac-Toe

Look at the boxes.
Put in the answers.
Color the **3** boxes with the same answer.

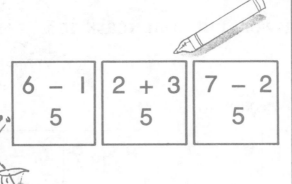

6 − 1	2 + 3	7 − 2
5	5	5

4 + 0	13 − 8	9 + 2
4		
7 − 3	6 + 4	10 + 1
	10	
10 − 2	3 + 5	13 − 5

You found tic-tac-toe.

Play again.

12 − 8	2 + 4	5 + 4
8 + 2	15 − 9	7 + 2
7 + 5	13 − 7	6 + 6

Tic-Tac-Toe

Play these tic-tac-toe games with a grown-up.

Play them just like all tic-tac-toe games.

Before you mark **X** or **O**, you must add or subtract.

If your answer is right, put your mark in the box.

If your answer is wrong, try again.

When you get the right answer, put your mark in the box.

Take turns. Try to mark **3** boxes in a row.

8 − 5	6 + 6	3 + 8
6 + 7	8 − 3	13 − 3
3 + 2	9 + 1	5 + 8

8 + 9	6 − 2	12 − 3
8 + 4	8 + 8	7 − 3
12 − 4	8 − 4	8 + 10

10 − 3	11 − 3	6 + 4
11 − 4	10 + 5	15 − 5
13 + 2	10 − 4	13 − 3

Adding and Subtracting with Basic Facts: Sums to 15

Add 10

Here is a game board.

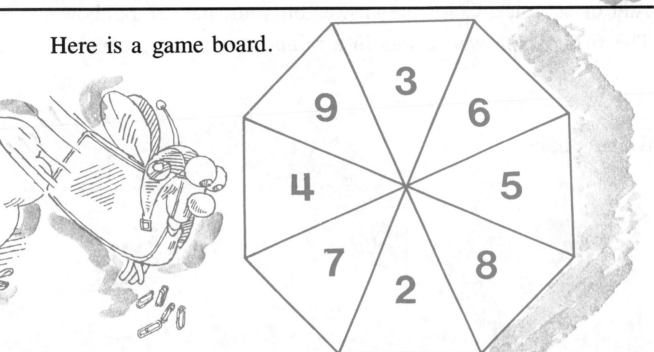

Drop a paper clip on the board.

What number did you get? _____

Add 10 to the number. $+10$

Write the sum. _____

Play again.

Write the number. _____

Add 10. _____

Write the sum. _____

What was your best score? _____

Play again.

Write the number. _____

Add 10. $+10$

Write the sum. _____

Play again.

Write the number. _____

Add 10. _____

Write the sum. _____

Rainbow Numbers

Play this game with a grown-up.

Toss a coin or a paper clip on the game board.
Add or subtract. Color the answer on your number rainbow.
The first person who colors in a rainbow wins the game.

Game Board

11-3	10+9	8+9	6+4	5+7	9+4
8+8	15-5	12-3	8+6	7+4	6+7

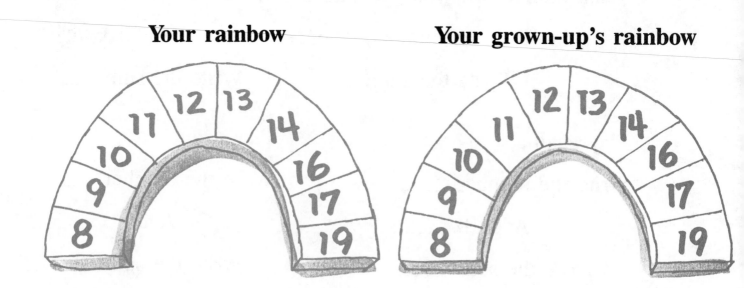

Your rainbow   **Your grown-up's rainbow**

Adding and Subtracting with Basic Facts: Sums to 19

Heads or Tails

Toss a coin.

Heads = 10 points.

Tails = 5 points.

Play the game.

Heads   Tails

Play again.

Toss 1 _____

Toss 2 _____

Toss 3 _____

   Add _____

Ring the answer.

15   20   25   30

Play again.

Toss 1 _____

Toss 2 _____

Toss 3 _____

   Add _____

Ring the answer.

15   20   25   30

Toss 1 _____

Toss 2 _____

Toss 3 _____

   Add _____

Ring the answer.

15   20   25   30

Play again.

Toss 1 _____

Toss 2 _____

Toss 3 _____

   Add _____

Ring the answer.

15   20   25   30

The 77 Game

Play this game with a grown-up.

Make number cards like these.

Pick a number card.   Your 77 board   Your grown-up's board

Write the number in a square.

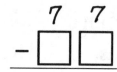   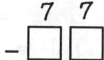

Pick another card.

Write the number in the other square.
Subtract.

Your grown-up does the same.

Who has the greater score?

_____

Hooray, the winner!

Play again with **88**.   Play again with **99**.

      Subtracting 2-Digit Numbers

The Square Family

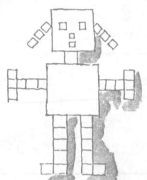

This is a square girl.

This is **not** a square girl.

Draw a square hat.

Draw a square house.

Draw a square dog.

Draw a square cat.

What Rolls?

Do this with a grown up.

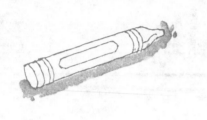

Can you roll a crayon?

Can you roll a shoe?

yes   no

yes   no

Which of these things can you roll? Find some and try it.

Draw things that roll.

Draw things that do not roll.

Can you roll yourself? _____

Identifying Attributes of Solid Figures

A Shape Hunt

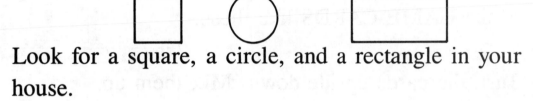

Look for a square, a circle, and a rectangle in your house.

Find a square.
Where was it? Make a drawing.

Find a circle.
Where was it? Make a drawing.

Find a rectangle. Where was it? Make a drawing.

Shape Game

Play this game with a grown-up.

Get a marker for each player. You can use a coin.

Put the markers on START.

Make GAME CARDS like these.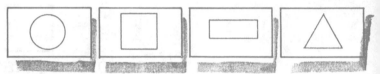

Turn the cards upside down. Mix them up.

Player 1 picks a card and moves his marker to that shape.

Replace the card. Mix up the cards again. Player 2 takes a turn. The first player to FINISH wins!

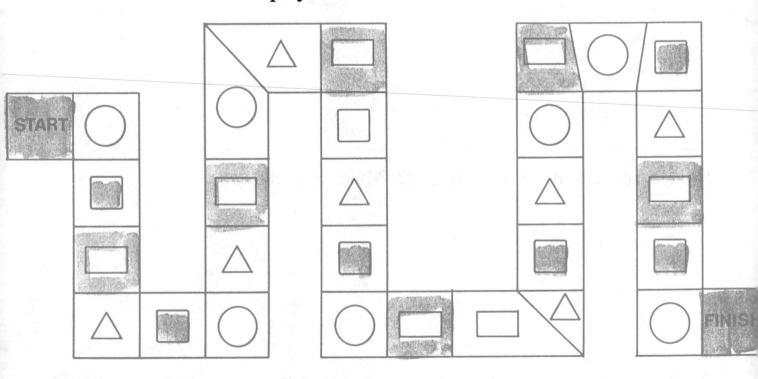

Identifying Squares, Rectangles, Circles and Triangles

A Pencil Long

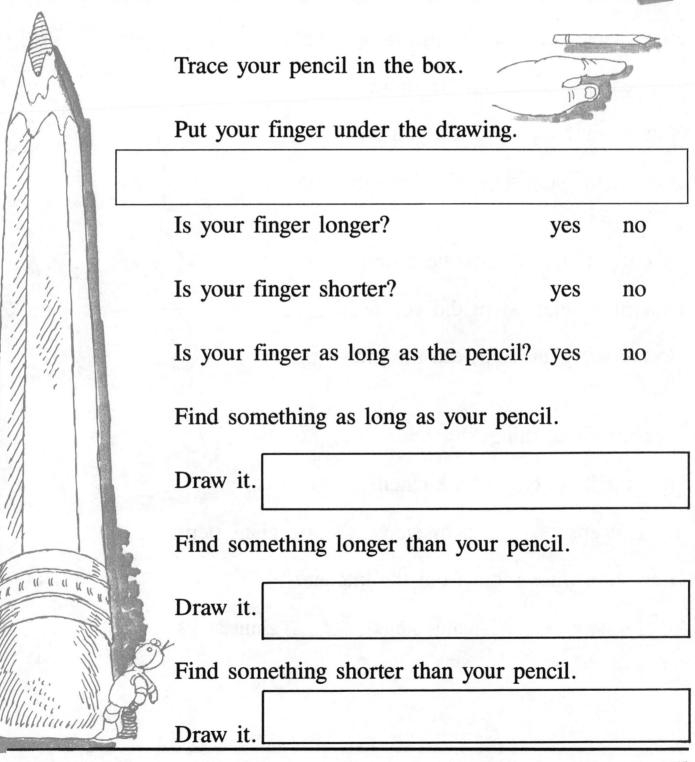

Trace your pencil in the box.

Put your finger under the drawing.

Is your finger longer?   yes   no

Is your finger shorter?   yes   no

Is your finger as long as the pencil? yes   no

Find something as long as your pencil.

Draw it.

Find something longer than your pencil.

Draw it.

Find something shorter than your pencil.

Draw it.

A Trip Across Your Room

Do this with a grown-up.

Walk across the room.

How many steps did you take? _____

How many steps did the grown-up take? _____

Take baby steps across the room.

How many baby steps did you take? _____

How many baby steps did the grown-up take? _____

Take giant steps across the room.

How many giant steps did you take? _____

How many giant steps did the grown-up take? _____

Measure other things.

How far is it across the kitchen?

_____ steps   _____ baby steps   _____ giant steps

How far is your room from the kitchen?

_____ steps   _____ baby steps   _____ giant steps

Measuring Length

Your Shoe

Trace your shoe here.

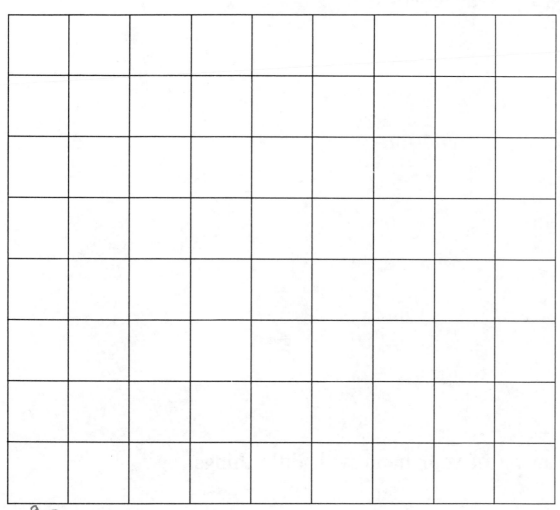

Color your drawing.

How many squares does your shoe touch? _____

Your Hand

Do this with a grown-up.

Trace your hand here.

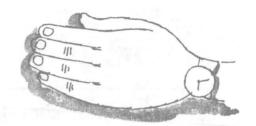

Keep your fingers together.

Cover the drawing of your hand with little things.

Use dried beans, noodles, or coins.

What did you use to cover your hand? _____

How many did you use to cover your hand? _____

Which is Heavier?

Hold a pencil in one hand.

Hold a cup in the other hand.

Which is heavier? Ring the answer.

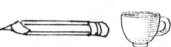

Hold a book in one hand.

Hold 3 spoons in the other hand.

Which is heavier?

Hold 3 spoons in one hand.

Hold a glass in the other hand.

Which is heavier?

Hold a plate in one hand.

Hold 2 forks in the other hand.

Which is heavier?

Fill it Up

Do this with a grown-up.

Get a big bowl.

Get a cup.

Fill the cup with water.

Pour the water into the bowl.

Fill the cup again.

Pour the water into the bowl.

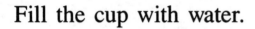

How many cups do you need to fill the bowl? _____

Ask your grown-up to try.

How many cups did your grown-up need? _____

Try this with a pot.   Try this with a pan.

Use the cup to fill a pot. Use the cup to fill a pan.

How many cups did you need? _____

How many cups did you need? _____

Clocks

Look at a clock or a watch

Ring the kind you have.

 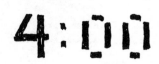

Show the time you see.

 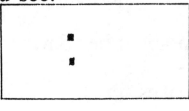

How many clocks and watches are in your house? _____

What do you like to eat in the morning? _____
Draw a picture.

What do you like to eat at night? _____
Draw a picture.

My Day

Do this with a grown-up.   Tell about your day.

I go to bed at _____ o'clock.

I wake up at _____ o'clock.

I eat breakfast at _____ o'clock.

I go to school at _____ o'clock.

I come home from school at _____ o'clock.

I eat dinner at _____ o'clock.

Ring your favorite time of day.

morning   afternoon   night

Ask a grown-up about her day.

My grown-up wakes up at _____ o'clock.

My grown-up eats breakfast at _____ o'clock.

My grown-up eats dinner at _____ o'clock.

My grown-up goes to bed at _____ o'clock.

Ring your grown-up's favorite time of day.

morning   afternoon   night

How Tall — How Long

Use your centimeter ruler for this page.

How tall is the girl?   **How tall is the boy?**

_____ centimeters   _____ centimeters

Who is taller?   girl   boy

How long is the pencil?   How long is the pen?

_____ centimeters   _____ centimeters

Which is longer?   pencil   pen

Guess How Long

Do this with a grown-up.

Use your centimeter ruler.

Look at the key. Guess how long it is?

Your guess: _____ centimeters

Your grown-up's guess: _____ centimeters

Measure and see. The key is _____ centimeters long.

Look at the thumb. Guess how long it is?

Your guess: _____ centimeters

Your grown-up's guess: _____ centimeters

Measure and see. The thumb is _____ centimeters long.

Guess how long your thumb is?

Your guess: _____ centimeters

Your grown-up's guess: _____ centimeters

Measure and see. Your thumb is _____ centimeters long.

Puzzle Parts

Part of the puzzle is missing.

Ring the missing part.

Part of the puzzle is missing.

Ring the missing part.

Numbers About Me

Do this with a grown-up.
You use numbers every day.
Fill in some special numbers that tell about you.

I am _____ years old.

My birthday is _____ .

My phone number is _____ .

My address is _____

_____ .

I have _____ stuffed animals.

My shoe size is _____ .

I can count up to _____ .

My lucky number is _____ .

My favorite TV show is on channel _____ .

Crazy Creatures

Here is a Fip.   Here are more Fips.

Here is a Boop.   Here are more Boops.

Are these Fips or Boops?   Fips   Boops

Are these Fips or Boops?   Fips   Boops

Draw a Fip.   Draw a Boop.

Your Kitchen

Do this with a grown-up.

Look around the kitchen.

Draw foods you drink.

Draw foods you chew.

Draw foods you like.

Draw a food you like and you chew.

Ask a grown-up to draw a food he likes and he chews.

Silly Pictures

Draw some silly pictures.

Draw a fat blue mouse with a red hat.

Draw a thin red mouse with a blue hat.

Draw a thin blue cat in a red hat playing with a fat red mouse.

Can You Find It?

Do this with a grown-up.

Try to find special things in your house.

Find something green and soft.

What is it? _____

Draw it.

Find something old and blue.

What is it? _____

Draw it.

Find something hard and red and new.

What is it? _____

Draw it.

Number Pictures

LESSON
30

Here is a **60** board.
Count by threes to **60.**
Start: 3, 6, 9, 12, 15.
Color these numbers
on the board.
Can you see a pattern?

1	2	3	4	5	6	7	8	9	10
11	12	13	14	15	16	17	18	19	20
21	22	23	24	25	26	27	28	29	30
31	32	33	34	35	36	37	38	39	40
41	42	43	44	45	46	47	48	49	50
51	52	53	54	55	56	57	58	59	60

Here is a **90** board.
Count by nines to **90.**
Start: 9, 18, 27, 36.
Color these numbers
on the board.
Can you see a pattern?

1	2	3	4	5	6	7	8	9	10
11	12	13	14	15	16	17	18	19	20
21	22	23	24	25	26	27	28	29	30
31	32	33	34	35	36	37	38	39	40
41	42	43	44	45	46	47	48	49	50
51	52	53	54	55	56	57	58	59	60
61	62	63	64	65	66	67	68	69	70
71	72	73	74	75	76	77	78	79	80
81	82	83	84	85	86	87	88	89	90

Finding Number Patterns and Skip Counting

Pattern Page

Do this with a grown-up.

Here are two pattern drawings.
They have different patterns.

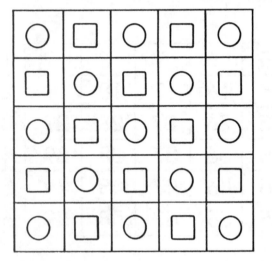 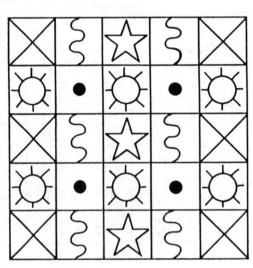

You can make a pattern drawing too.
Use colors or shapes in your drawing.
Ask a grown-up to make a drawing too.

My pattern drawing

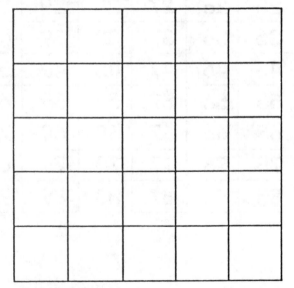

My grown-up's pattern drawing

Making Patterns

Colored Boxes

Get a blue crayon 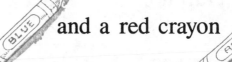 and a red crayon   .

Here are 4 boxes. Color them.

RED	BLUE
BLUE	RED

Here are 4 more boxes. Color them.

RED	RED
RED	BLUE

Color these 4 boxes in a new way.

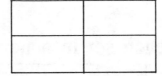

Here are more boxes. Color each set in a new way.

More Colored Boxes

Do this with a grown-up.

Get a blue crayon   Get a red crayon

Get a green crayon

Here are **3** boxes. Color them.

BLUE	RED	GREEN

Here are **3** more boxes. Color them.

BLUE	BLUE	GREEN

Color these **3** boxes in a new way.

Here are more boxes. Color each set in a new way.

| | | | | | | |
|--|--|--| |--|--|--|

| | | | | | | |
|--|--|--| |--|--|--|

| | | | | | | |
|--|--|--| |--|--|--|

| | | | | | | |
|--|--|--| |--|--|--|

Using Logical Thinking and Organizing Information

Enrichment
MATH

Grade 1
Answer Key and Teaching Suggestions

AMERICAN EDUCATION PUBLISHING

OVERVIEW

ENRICHMENT MATH was developed to provide children with additional opportunities to practice and review mathematical concepts and skills and to use these skills in the home. Children work individually on the first page of each lesson and then with family members on the second page. Every lesson presents high interest activities designed to heighten children's awareness of mathematical ideas and to enrich their understanding of those ideas.

ENRICHMENT MATH consists of 31 two page lessons at grade levels 1 through 6. At each grade level *ENRICHMENT MATH* covers all of the important topics of the traditional mathematics curriculum. Each lesson is filled with games, puzzles and other opportunities for exploring mathematical ideas.

AUTHORS

Peggy Kaye is the author of *Games For Math* and *Games for Reading*. She spent ten years as a classroom teacher in New York City public and private schools, and is today a private tutor in math and reading.

Carole Greenes is Professor of Mathematics at Boston University. She has taught mathematics and mathematics education for more than 20 years and is a former elementary school teacher. Dr. Greenes is the author of a K-8 basal math series and has also written for programs such as *Reach Program, Trivia Math* and the *TOPS-Problem*.

Linda Schulman is Professor of Mathematics at Lesley College . For the past 12 years, she has taught courses in mathematics and mathematics education. Prior to her work at the college level, Dr. Schulman taught elementary school. She is the author of a basal mathematics textbook as well as of other curriculum programs including *TOPS-Problem Solving Program, The Mathworks* and *How to Solve Story Problems*.

WHY ENRICHMENT MATH?

Enrichment and parental involvement are both crucial parts of children's education. More school systems are recognizing that this part of the educational process is crucial to school success. Enrichment activities give children the opportunity to practice basic skills and that encourages them to think mathematically. That's exactly the kind of opportunity children get when doing *ENRICHMENT MATH*.

One of the important goals of *ENRICHMENT MATH* is to increase children's involvement in mathematics and mathematical concepts. When children are involved in mathematics activities, they become more alert and receptive to learning. They understand more. They remember more. Games, puzzles, and "hands-on" activities that lead to mathematical discoveries are guaranteed to get children involved in mathematics. That's why such activities form the core of each *ENRICHMENT MATH* lesson.

Another important goal of *ENRICHMENT MATH* is to provide opportunities for parents to become involved in their children's education. Every *ENRICHMENT MATH* lesson has two parts. First, there is a lesson that the children do on their own. Second, there is a game or an activity that the child does with an adult. *ENRICHMENT MATH* doesn't ask parents to teach children. Instead the program asks parents to play math games and engage in interesting math activities with their children.

Published in 1995 by AMERICAN EDUCATION PUBLISHING
© 1991 SRA/McGraw-Hill

HOW TO USE ENRICHMENT MATH

Each *ENRICHMENT MATH* book consists of 31 lessons on perforated sheets. On the front of each sheet, there is an activity that the child completes independently. On the back there is a follow-up activity for the child to complete with an adult. These group activities include games, projects, puzzles, surveys and trivia quizzes. The front and back pages of a lesson focus on the same mathematical skill.

Activities may be done at the time the skills are being taught to provide additional practice, or used at a later date to maintain skill levels.

Within each book, the lessons are organized into four or five sections. These sections correspond to the major mathematical topics emphasized at the particular grade level. This means you can quickly locate a lesson on whatever topic you want at whatever level is appropriate for your child. Let's say your first-grader is working on addition in school. You can feel confident that the first several lessons in the addition and subtraction section will have something suited to your needs.

Also Available—ENRICHMENT READING

Overview

ENRICHMENT READING is designed to provide children with practice in reading and to increase their reading abilities. The program consists of six books, one each for grade levels 1 through 6. The major areas of reading instruction—word skills, vocabulary, study skills, and literary forms—are covered as appropriate at each level.

ENRICHMENT READING provides a wide range of activities that target a variety of skills in each instructional area. The program is unique because it helps children expand their skills in playful ways with games, puzzles, riddles, contests, and stories. The high-interest activities are informative and fun to do.

Home and parental involvement is important to any child's success in school. *ENRICHMENT READING* is the ideal vehicle for fostering home involvement. Every lesson provides specific opportunities for children to work with a parent, a family member, an adult, or a friend.

LOOK FOR *ENRICHMENT READING* and *ENRICHMENT MATH* at stores that carry Master Skills.

Also Available from American Education Publishing—

BRIGHTER CHILD™ SOFTWARE

The Brighter Child™ Software series is a set of innovative programs designed to teach basic reading, phonics, and math skills in a fun and engaging way to children ages 3 - 9.

Muppet™/Brighter Child™ Software available on CD-ROM

*Same & Different	Sorting & Ordering
*Letters: Capital & Small	Thinking Skills
*Beginning Sounds: Phonics	Sound Patterns: More Phonics

also available on diskette

Brighter Child™ Software available on CD-ROM and diskette

Math Grade 1	Math Grade 2	Math Grade 3
Reading Grade 1	Reading Grade 2	Reading Grade 3

●**call (800) 542-7833 for more information**

Brighter Child™ Software Available at Stores Near You

TEACHING SUGGESTIONS
Grade 1
Optional Activities

A TIP FOR SUCCESS

First graders will find *ENRICHMENT MATH* activities easy to understand. Each lesson has simple instructions and ample pictorial aides. Nevertheless, you may want to spend a few minutes explaining the lessons before having your child complete them. You might even play some of the games prior to giving your child the lessons. The games will liven up math time and prepare your child for success.

Part One: Counting and Place Value

ENRICHMENT MATH has 9 lessons on counting and place value. You can use the first lessons early in the school year. Wait to give the lessons at the end of this section, though, until your child is familiar with place value concepts.

Counting is the foundation on which children build all future math skills. The lessons in *ENRICHMENT MATH* help solidify this foundation. Doing these lessons, the youngsters will count knives, people in their family, doors, even sinks. Before doing the lessons, you can ask your child to estimate how many knives or doors they'll find at home. You can record the estimates and compare them later with the actual counts. After your child has finished these lessons, you'll have collected considerable data concerning your household. Try using this information to make bar graphs comparing sinks to doors and doors to people.

Here's another idea: take a counting tour of your home. Find out the number of coats in the closet, number of windows in your home, the number of pencils on Dad's desk. This activity can prime your child for the lessons, or make a good follow-up after counting at home.

A number of the lessons involve skip-counting by twos, fives, or tens. You can prepare your child for this with skip-counting contests. Challenge your child to clean up his or her bedroom before you count to sixty by twos or one hundred by tens. Be sure to count slowly.

Several lessons call for your child to count large collections (stars on a page, beans in a spoon). Try finding out the number of dried lima beans needed to fill a yogurt container. When the container is full, have your child count the beans one by one. After this, have your child take the same beans and group them by tens. Your child can record how many groups of ten there are and how many singles are left over. Compare the two kinds of counts. This will help your child understand place value.

Part Two: Addition and Subtraction

Children should have real objects to manipulate when they start adding and subtracting. That's why so many *ENRICHMENT MATH* lessons have children add sets of pennies or paper clips or draw pictures before solving problems.

The middle lessons in this section call for children to add and subtract without assigning concrete materials as aids. First graders, however, should feel free to use any counting tool they want, like fingers, beans, Unifix cubes, etc.

Some lessons in Part Two help children understand the commutative property of addition. Children who understand that $3 + 5$ gives the same sum as $5 + 3$ can memorize the addition table in half the time. A few lessons help children see the relationship between $3 + 5 = 8$ and $8 - 5 = 3$. Children who appreciate the connection between addition and subtraction have an easier time learning their subtraction facts. What's more, these children gain real insight into the intricacies of the number system.

Part Two is filled with games.

Part Three: Geometry and Measurement

Part Three is a grab bag of activities covering the major themes in first grade geometry and measurement curriculum. These lessons are well within the range of first graders, even at the beginning of the year.

When children share homework results, it increases their interest in the activities. After completing *What Rolls?* (page 42), for instance, your child might enjoy making a giant chart listing the things he or she rolled at home. Look in other places for more objects that roll. Add them to the chart.

Have a discussion about the difference between baby steps and giant steps or between grown-up steps and child steps. Try taking giant step measurements of your home. Can you tell from the count who has the longest stride?

Try *Your Hand* (page 48). Only this time have your child use two or three different objects to cover their hand drawings. Does the size of the object affect the results?

Part Four: Mathematical Thinking

In Part Four you'll find a variety of activities that help children think logically, observe patterns, develop spatial awareness, and discover the many roles numbers play in our lives. These activities aren't numerical or geometrical, but they do help first graders expand their mathematical abilities.

Since answers vary for Grade 1, there is no answer key.

Also Available—ENRICHMENT READING

Overview

ENRICHMENT READING is designed to provide children with practice in reading and to increase their reading abilities. The program consists of six books, one each for grade levels 1 through 6. The major areas of reading instruction—word skills, vocabulary, study skills, and literary forms—are covered as appropriate at each level.

ENRICHMENT READING provides a wide range of activities that target a variety of skills in each instructional area. The program is unique because it helps children expand their skills in playful ways with games, puzzles, riddles, contests, and stories. The high-interest activities are informative and fun to do.

Home and parental involvement is important to any child's success in school. ENRICHMENT READING is the ideal vehicle for fostering home involvement. Every lesson provides specific opportunities for children to work with a parent, a family member, an adult, or a friend.

LOOK FOR **ENRICHMENT READING** and **ENRICHMENT MATH** at stores that carry Master Skills.

MASTER SKILLS SERIES SKILL BOOKS

Completely edited for Spring 1995!
Additional Enrichment Section included!

The Master Skills Series is not just another work-book series! These full-color workbooks were conceived and designed by experts who are also parents...parents who understand the value of reinforcing basic skills!

This exciting series has drawn national acclaim for its highly illustrated, contemporary lessons and challenging content. Parents are also noticing a difference in their child's perfor-mance in school. It's true...the involvement of a parent in the learning process makes it much more dynamic and interesting for the child.

Also included is an 8-page section of material from our newest series, Enrichment Reading and Enrichment Math! (Enrichment section not included in Grade K Books)

READING SKILL BOOKS
Grade K Reading - EXPANDED!
Grade 1 Reading
Grade 2 Reading
Grade 3 Reading
Grade 4 Reading
Grade 5 Reading
Grade 6 Reading

MATH SKILL BOOKS
Grade K Math - EXPANDED!
Grade 1 Math
Grade 2 Math
Grade 3 Math
Grade 4 Math
Grade 5 Math
Grade 6 Math

ENGLISH SKILL BOOKS
Grade K English - EXPANDED!
Grade 1 English
Grade 2 English
Grade 3 English
Grade 4 English
Grade 5 English
Grade 6 English

THINKING SKILLS SKILL BOOKS
Grade 1 Thinking Skills
Grade 2 Thinking Skills
Grade 3 Thinking Skills
Grade 4 Thinking Skills
Grade 5 Thinking Skills
Grade 6 Thinking Skills

COMPREHENSION SKILL BOOKS
Grade K Early Learning Skills – NEW!
Grade 1 Comprehension
Grade 2 Comprehension
Grade 3 Comprehension
Grade 4 Comprehension
Grade 5 Comprehension
Grade 6 Comprehension

SPELLING & WRITING SKILL BOOKS
Grade 1 Spelling & Writing
Grade 2 Spelling & Writing
Grade 3 Spelling & Writing
Grade 4 Spelling & Writing
Grade 5 Spelling & Writing
Grade 6 Spelling & Writing

INTRODUCING
BRIGHTER CHILD™ SOFTWARE!

BRIGHTER CHILD ™ SOFTWARE for Windows

These colorful and exciting programs teach basic skills in an entertaining way. They are based on the best selling BRIGHTER CHILD™ workbooks, written and designed by experts who are also parents. Sound is included to facilitate learning, but it is not nesessary to run these programs. BRIGHTER CHILD™ software has received many outstanding reviews and awards. All Color! Easy to use!

The following programs are each sold separately in a 3.5 disk format.

Reading & Phonics Grade 1   Reading Grade 2   Reading Grade 3
Math Grade 1   Math Grade 2   Math Grade 3

CD-ROM Titles!

These new titles combine three grade levels of a subject on one CD-ROM! Each CD contains more than 80 different activities packed with colors and sound.

Reading and Phonics Challenge - CD-ROM Grades 1, 2, 3
Math Challenge - CD-ROM Grades 1, 2, 3

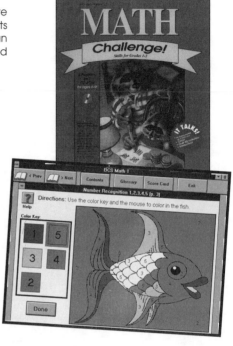

JIM HENSON'S MUPPET™/
BRIGHTER CHILD™ SOFTWARE for Windows™

Based on the best selling Muppet Press™/BRIGHTER CHILD™ Workbooks, these software programs for Windows are designed to teach basic concepts to children in preschool and kindergarten. Children will develop phonics skills and critical and creative thinking skills, and more! No reading is required with a sound card -- the directions are read aloud. The Muppet™ characters are universally known and loved and are recognized as having high educational value.

The following programs are each sold separately in a 3.5 disk format.
Each package contains:

- a program disk with more than 15 full color animated interactive lessons!
- sound is included which facilitates learning.
- Full-color workbook

Beginning Sounds: Phonics   Letters: Capital & Small
Same & Different

CD-ROM Titles

Beginning Reading & Phonics- CD-ROM

This title combines three different MUPPET™/BRIGHTER CHILD™ Software programs -- Beginning Sounds: Phonics, Letters, and Same and Different -- all on one CD-ROM! This valuable software contains more than 50 different activities packed with color, sound, and interactive animation!

Reading & Phonics II- CD-ROM

Three Muppet™ Early Reading Programs on one CD-ROM. Includes *Sorting & Ordering*, *Thinking Skills*, and *Sound Patterns: More Phonics*

Available at stores everywhere.

NOTES